MW01288666

The Great Chicago Fire of 1871: The Story of the Blaze That Destroyed the Midwest's Largest City

By Charles River Editors

Harper's Weekly illustration of the Great Chicago Fire

About Charles River Editors

Charles River Editors provides superior editing and original writing services across the digital publishing industry, with the expertise to create digital content for publishers across a vast range of subject matter. In addition to providing original digital content for third party publishers, we also republish civilization's greatest literary works, bringing them to new generations of readers via ebooks.

Sign up here to receive updates about free books as we publish them, and visit Our Kindle Author Page to browse today's free promotions and our most recently published Kindle titles.

Introduction

Picture of the ruins at Dearborn and Monroe

The Great Chicago Fire of 1871

"The fire was barely fifteen minutes old. What followed was a series of fatal errors that set the fire free and doomed the city to a fiery death." – Jim Murphy, *The Great Fire*

It had taken about 40 years for Chicago to grow from a small settlement of about 300 people into a thriving metropolis with a population of 300,000, but in just two days in 1871, much of that progress was burned to the ground. In arguably the most famous fire in American history, a blaze in the southwestern section of Chicago began to burn out of control on the night of October 8, 1871. Thanks to *The Chicago Tribune*, the fire has been apocryphally credited to a cow kicking over a lantern in Mrs. Catherine O'Leary's barn, and though that was not true, the rumor dogged Mrs. O'Leary to the grave.

Of course, the cause of the fire didn't matter terribly much to the people who lost their lives or their property in the blaze. Thanks to dry conditions, wind, and wooden buildings, firefighters were never actually able to stop the fire, which burned itself out only after it spent nearly two whole days incinerating several square miles of Chicago. By the time rain mercifully helped to put the fire out, the Great Chicago Fire had already killed an estimated 300 people, destroyed an estimated 17,500 buildings, and left nearly 100,000 people (1/3 of the population) homeless.

Several other theories have developed as an explanation for the fire. Most of them center on people around Mrs. O'Leary's barn, but other have gone so far as to blame a meteor shower as the culprit that started fires across the Midwest that same night. As proof, they note that the country's worst forest fire in history took place around the same time in the logging town of Peshtigo in northeastern Wisconsin, a fire that killed thousands.

Mrs. O'Leary and her barn remain a part of lore, but it also speaks to Chicago's ability to rebuild that it's almost impossible to envision a farm in downtown Chicago today. Chicago suffered a wide swath of destruction, but it had rebuilt itself within 20 years in order to host the World's Fair, evidence that it was back and bigger and better than ever. Along with that, Chicago has maintained its status as the region's biggest city and one of the most important in America.

The Great Chicago Fire chronicles one of the largest natural disasters of the 19th century in America. Along with pictures of important people, places, and events, you will learn about the Great Chicago Fire of 1871 like never before, in no time at all.

The Great Chicago Fire of 1871: The Story of the Blaze That Destroyed the Midwest's Largest City

About Charles River Editors

Introduction

Chapter 1: The O'Leary Legend

A map showing the section of Chicago that burned in the fire, with Mrs. O'Leary's barn marked by a red dot in the southwestern part of the damaged section.

"I was in bed myself and my husband and five children when this fire commenced. I was the owner of them five cows that was burnt, and the horse wagon and harness. I had two tons of coal and two tons of hay. I had everything that I wanted in for the winter. I could not save five cents worth of anything out of the barn. Only that Mr. Sullivan got out a little calf. The calf was worth eleven dollars on Saturday morning. Saturday morning I refused even eleven dollars for the calf, and it was sold afterwards for eight dollars. I didn't save five cents out of the fire. I could not tell anything of the fire only that two men came by the door. I guess it was my husband got outside the door and he ran back to the bedroom and said 'Kate the barn is afire.' I ran out and the whole barn was on fire. Well I went out to the barn and upon my word I could not tell anyone about the fire. I got just the way I could not tell anything about the fire." - Catherine O'Leary

Although people who have only passing familiarity with the Great Chicago Fire often know the legend about Mrs. O'Leary's cow, little is actually known for certain about how the fire began. It was pretty clear that the fire began a short while after 9:00 p.m. on Sunday evening, October 8, 1871, but even before the last flame had died down, a colorful legend had grown up around the cause of the fire. While there were many different versions of the original story, the gist of it was that Kate O'Leary went out after dark to care for or check on her cows, and for some reason, she left the kerosene lantern she was carrying with her in the barn. Then, after she went back into the house, one of her cows kicked it over, spilling the oil and igniting the hay.

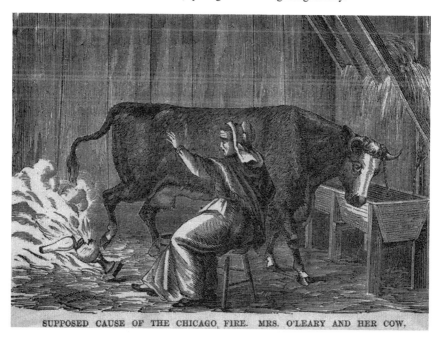

SUPPOSED CAUSE OF THE CHICAGO FIRE. MRS. O'LEARY AND HER COW.

A *Harper's Magazine* illustration depicting O'Leary and her cow

Although the legend sounds fanciful today, there were several reasons why the story seemed plausible to investigators. First, according to the board who reviewed the evidence, "the fire originated in a two-story barn in the rear of No. 137 DeKoven Street, the premises being owned by Patrick O'Leary. The fire was first discovered by a drayman by the name of Daniel [Dennis] Sullivan, who saw it while sitting on the sidewalk on the south side of DeKoven Street, and nearly opposite O'Leary's premises. He fixes the time at not more than twenty or twenty-five minutes past nine o'clock when he first noticed the flames coming out of the barn. There is no proof that any person had been in the barn after nightfall that evening. Whether it originated from a spark blown from a chimney on that windy night, or was set on fire by human agency, we are unable to determine. Mr. O'Leary and all his family prove to have been in bed and asleep at the time. There was a small party in the front part of O'Leary's house, which was occupied by Mr. McLaughlin and wife. But we fail to find any evidence that anybody from McLaughlin's part of the house went near the barn that night." Furthermore, the O'Leary's did keep cows in that barn, and the cows would have needed care on the farm.

The O'Leary house at No. 137 DeKoven Street

However, except in the case of a cow giving birth, there would be no reason for anyone to have gone to the barn at night. Milking was done in the morning and the evening, but always during daylight hours, meaning there would have been no reason for Mrs. O'Leary to leave a lighted lamp in the barn. Not only would it potentially start a fire, it would also waste oil, which the O'Leary's could not afford to waste.

Of course, the most damning evidence refuting the story came from the man who originally published it. 22 years later, Michael Ahern publically admitted that he had added the story to his original article on the fire to lend some local color to the event.

If indeed the fire was started as a result of someone or something on the O'Leary farm, there were better suspects than Mrs. O'Leary or her cows. According to O'Leary's testimony before the board investigating the fire, there was quite a party going on in another part of the house that night. The family had rented two front rooms to the McLaughlin's, who were the ones throwing the party, and while O'Leary maintained that she was not in attendance, she claimed she could hear what was going on. This led to speculation on some people's parts that there was also gambling going on in the barn, which would at least would present a plausible reason for there being a lit lamp out there. Someone could have knocked it over, especially if there was alcohol involved, and then chose to run rather than try to put it out. In fact, according to an article published decades later, Louis Cohn, then a well-respected world traveler, was honored by Northwestern University's Medill School of Journalism for his large contribution to the college, Cohn maintained for years that he was responsible for the fire: "Mr. Cohn had an interesting connection with the origin of the Great Chicago Fire. He steadfastly maintained that the traditional story of the cause of the fire -- Mrs. O'Leary's cow that kicked over a lantern -- was untrue. He asserted that he and Mrs. O'Leary's son, in the company of several other boys, were shooting dice in the hayloft . . . by the light of a lantern, when one of the boys accidently overturned the lantern, thus setting the barn afire. Mr. Cohn never denied that when the other boys fled, he stopped long enough to scoop up the money."

While O'Leary and Louie Cohn have stories that offer a down-to-earth explanation for the fire, Ignatius Donnelly had a much more heavenly explanation. He speculated that the fire was caused by a meteor shower created when Biela's comet lost its tail. In defending his theory, he pointed accurately to other fires that broke out at that time around the Midwest: "At that hour, half past nine o'clock in the evening, at apparently the same moment, at points hundreds of miles apart, in three different States, Wisconsin, Michigan, and Illinois, fires of the most peculiar and devastating kind broke out, so far as we know, by spontaneous combustion. In Wisconsin, on its eastern borders, in a heavily timbered country, near Lake Michigan, a region embracing four hundred square miles, extending north from Brown County, and containing Peshtigo, Manistee, Holland, and numerous villages on the shores of Green Bay, was swept bare by an absolute whirlwind of flame. There were seven hundred and fifty people killed outright, besides great numbers of the wounded, maimed, and burned, who died afterward. More than three million dollars' worth of property was destroyed." While the meteorite explanation still has a number of defenders, it has never gained wide spread popularity in the scientific community.

Chapter 2: Wood, Wind and Fire

"This season has been the dryest in the West for years. We hadn't had a drop of rain for months, and there had been but one cloudy day during the month of September. The result was that the dust was almost intolerable, the ground became parched, and the houses were as dry as tinder. Besides a furious wind from the southwest had been blowing steadily all day Sunday, one of the most violent winds I ever saw in a clear day." - William Gallagher

Though the fire ultimately spread out of control, the fire department reported that it was able to respond immediately to the reported blaze: "The first information received by the Fire Department came from the alarm struck in the fire-alarm office at 9:30. The alarm sounded Box No. 342, at the corner of Canalport Avenue and Halsted Street, a point in the direction of the fire, but a mile beyond it. There was no signal given by any box to the central office, but the box was given by Mathias Schaffer, from the Court house cupola, he being the night watchman on duty at the time, and having sighted the fire. There was no signal given from anybody until after the Fire Department had arrived and turned in the second and third alarms. If any person set the fire, either by accident or design, he was careful not to give the alarm. The nearest engine-house was six blocks from the fire; the next nearest one was nine blocks away. The nearest hose-house was located eleven blocks from the fire, and, at this hose-house, the watchman had seen the fire before the alarm was given from the Court House, and the company were on their way to the fire before the box was struck."

The Courthouse after the fire

The problem was that Chicago was the scene of a perfect storm of circumstances that conspired together to spread the fire. First, there were the houses themselves; at that time, wood was still the favorite choice of building material in the Midwest, and more than half of all the structures in Chicago were made of wood. Furthermore, even the city's sidewalks were made of wood, providing excellent paths for the fire to travel on from one building to the next. Writing a month after the catastrophe, noted architect Frederick Olmsted blamed the way in which the city constructed its large building for helping spread the fire: "Some ostensibly stone fronts had huge overhanging wooden or sheet-metal cornices fastened directly to their roof timbers, with wooden parapets above them. Flat roofs covered with tarred felt and pebbles were common. In most cases, I am told by observers, the fire entered the great buildings by their roof timbers, even common sheet-metal seeming to offer but slight and very temporary protection to the wood on which it rested. Plain brick walls or walls of brick with solid stone quoins and window-dressings evidently resisted the fire much better than stone-faced walls with a thin backing of brick."

Frederick Olmsted

That said, if the weather and season had been normal, it is unlikely that the fire would have gotten out of hand. Unfortunately, Chicago and much of the Midwest had suffered a severe drought during the summer of 1871, as meteorologists recorded just one inch of rainfall between July 4 and the day of the fire. The effects were still being felt, even in the cities. People had gone from making random comments about the heat to asking each other how long it'd been since it rained. As the drought continued, people started remarking about how important it was to be careful with fire. Public service announcements followed that, with everyone warned to be on the lookout for fire.

Of course, it was impossible during the 19th century to avoid using fire altogether. After all, every morning began with building a fire in the cook stove to make breakfast, and every evening ended around a kerosene lamp or, in wealthier homes, gaslight. In between, fire was used to keep homes warm and even to power steam engines in factories. At the same time, since most people lived with fire all the time, they were more comfortable with it, which could lead to additional care or to carelessness. In October 1871, it may have been the latter.

In addition to the drought, there was also the matter of wind that night. One fireman later wrote, "When they arrived there from three to five buildings were fiercely burning. The fire must have been burning from ten to fifteen minutes; and with the wind then blowing strongly from the southwest, and carrying the fire from building to building in a neighborhood composed wholly of dry wooden buildings, with wood shavings piled in every barn and under every house, the fire had got under too great headway for the engines called out by the first alarm to be able to subdue it...Marshal Williams immediately ordered the second, and, soon afterward, the third, alarm to be turned in, but ... before this could be accomplished, the strong wind had scattered the fire into the many buildings, all as dry as tinder, and spread it over so large an area that the whole Department ... were unable to cut it off or prevent the wind, which soon became a gale, from carrying burning shingles and brands over their heads, and setting on fire buildings far away from the main fire."

Finally, there was the matter of how close the buildings were to each other. In 1871, Chicago was in the middle of a huge growth spurt as people flocked to the city looking for work. Many were veterans of the Civil War who had growing families and needed places to live. Unable to afford much land, they built rambling houses on small lots, making the best use of the space possible. As a result, many neighboring rooftops nearly touched each other, making it easy for fires to leap from one building to the next.

Chapter 3: The Circumstances Were Terrifying

"[I]t was Sunday night after evening church that the sky became red again in the southwest, and rumors of a big fire in that direction were circulated. Soon it was heard that the Fire Department had lost control of it; and as there had been a drought, and as a large part of Chicago consisted of wooden buildings, there was a good deal of alarm felt. The four younger children were in bed, Lida and I in one room, and Dora and Emily in another. The rest of the family was in the library with neighbors who were watching the fire with them from the windows…The sky kept getting red and redder; the wind, already high, was increasing with the heat, and huge burning cinders were settling in every direction…Mother became very worried about Father, because it was after midnight; the fire was sweeping nearer; refugees loaded with goods were going north by our house; and altogether the circumstances were terrifying." - Ada Rumsey

In the years leading up to the fire, the city had grown to the point of averaging two fires a day somewhere in the area, but this was not overwhelming since the fire department was well-equipped with 17 horse drawn engines and staffed with more than 180 men. However, the frequency with which they were able to put out fires led to a certain complacency on the part of some of the firefighters, including the two Otis brothers. Their sister, Jennie, later recalled, "The room I occupied faced the west, being the back of the house. My two older brothers having the front room on the same floor. I had only been asleep a short while when I was awakened by the fire bells, which we had in those days, and the clanging of engines. My room windows had no shades, but inside blinds. As they were open, I saw the first of this west side fire. The wind was very strong from the south-west, blowing the flames toward the lake and the north side. It grew larger and larger, and after an hour I decided to go and call my brothers. As they had been to the fire the night before and were tired, they did not seem interested, and I returned to my room again, watched the fire leaping and spreading at a terrific rate. In a short while I decided to go again to my brothers' room; this time I was told to go back to bed and forget it."

Tragically, the fire her brothers had fought the night before had also been worked on by many other members of the Chicago Fire Department, leaving them exhausted. This was an important fact to keep in mind when examining any mistakes that may have been made, especially since many members of the department were called upon to give as much as 48 hours of uninterrupted service to very strenuous work, all while being tasked with attempting to use good judgment in making decisions on a scale they had never experienced before.

Though the men were able to put out the initial fire at the O'Leary barn, it had spread to other buildings before they were done. The firemen then changed their tactics and swung their engines around in an effort to stop the fire from the north, but by the time they got to their new location, sometime around 10:30, the fire was already ahead of them and forced them to fall back and move north again. By this time, their efforts were being hampered by the crowds of people flying into the streets and fleeing from the fire with whatever they could carry. Clarence Burley encountered these crowds himself and later recalled, "As I reached Kinzie Street I saw that flames were leaping across Clark Street some blocks South of the river. Many people were coming across the bridge. I thought the tunnel would be a better way to get to the other side. I found the foot passage of the tunnel full of people, with bundles and trunks of belongings, and just as I reached the entrance the gas went out."

Meanwhile, most of the citizens and visitors to Chicago continued to go about their business as if nothing was amiss. The latter group included Alfred Hebard and his family, who were only passing through Chicago and were spending the night at the Palmer Hotel. The building had been open to the public for less than two weeks, and Mrs. Hebard later described the scene: "Returning from an evening [church] service, we were told that another fire had broken out in the western part of the city and was progressing rapidly. We immediately took the elevator to the upper story of the Palmer, saw the fire, but, deciding that it would not cross the river, descended to our rooms in the second story to prepare for sleep. Husband and daughter soon retired; I remained up to prepare for the morrow's journey, and thus gain a little time for shopping before the departure of the train at 11 A.M. Feeling somewhat uneasy, I frequently opened the blinds, and each time found the light in the streets increased until every spire and dome seemed illuminated. I aroused my husband, asking him to go out and investigate once more, which he did, telling me, on his return, not to be alarmed, as there was no danger in our locality."

A picture of the Palmer House before the fire

By around 11:30 PM, the fire had spread well past DeKoven Street and was approaching the Chicago River. At this point, firefighters could only hope that the river itself was wide enough to stop the blaze from spreading any more, and they were encouraged by the fact that the previous night's fire had been in the same area, so much of what might fuel the current fire was already gone. However, their hopes were soon dashed as the bridges themselves caught fire and sent it across the water to the lumber yards and warehouses on the other side. Sparks and the debris from the fire also blew across the river and began landing on other structures, among them the South Side Gas Works. One witness remembered, "The fire on the West Side was fast burning to a point where it must stop--on the grounds burned over the night previous, when all at once the

South Side caught, near or at the Gas Works. I would have gone over then--had just seen the C & N Freight houses burn--but wanted the gas works to blow up before I went among the high stone buildings of the South Side. In less than half an hour I went over, after the explosion, and the whole portion of the South Side seemed to be on fire--all west of Dearborn. The burning shingle, pieces of lumber, paper roofing and every conceivable thing came rushing down through the air like snow, all was smoke and sparks and the wind would gather them up again building in huge windows for coals."

Chapter 4: Across the River

The Crosby Opera House before the fire

"Half past one Monday morning we were awakened by a loud knocking at the front door we were awake in an instant and dressing ourselves we looked about and saw a perfect shower of sparks flying over our house. I got some water and went out in the yard while my brother went up on the roof we worked for one or two hours at the end of that time we had to give up. We tried to get a wagon but could not so we put two trunks on a wheelbarrow and each of us shouldered a bundle and we marched for the old skating park I leading my goat. We got along very well until the Peshtigo Lumber yard caught on fire then it was all we could do to breathe. Mother caught on fire once but we put it out. At last we heard that there was a little shanty that hadn't burnt down so we marched there but had to leave our trunks and everything else but Charlie and father went back and got one but could not get the other as the sand was blowing in their faces and cut like glass at last a wagon drove up and we all piled in and escaped…" - Justin Butterfield

The loss of the gas plant only made things even more dangerous for those still trying to survive in the fire's path. In large cities like Chicago at the time, most of the larger houses were lit by gas lighting that was pumped to the houses by the station, so when the station was gone, people were forced to resort other sources of light, even while they continued to try to keep their homes from burning By this time, Alfred Hebard and his family had reached the home of their friends the Hubbard's and joined a large number of people taking refuge there. Mrs. Hebard explained, "The fire, meanwhile, was coming nearer, and just as we began in earnest to pack necessary things for removal, the Gasworks were destroyed and candles had to be resorted to. Everyone thought the house might be saved, standing as it did on a corner and disconnected from every other building, but we worked on through the night, preparing for the worst, and running often to the garret to see if the worst was not over. In the early morning men came, tore up carpets to cover the roof, draining both cisterns to keep the carpets wet, hoping if possible to stop the fire at that corner. Oh, how they worked! The thoughtful family provided refreshments as long as it was possible, and when all supplies were exhausted the men labored on, panting and parched with thirst, drinking the very dregs of the cistern water from tubs in the kitchen as they passed through. All said, 'This house will not burn!' but they might as well have tried to quench Vesuvius The heat increased. A wooden block nearby flashed into flame, and at 11 A.M. the cornice was blazing, and we were obliged to go out through the alley to escape the heat and cinders; but where to go we could not tell."

Once the fire jumped the river, it was obvious that the fire department would not be able to stop it. Furthermore, the wind itself had become so hot as a result of the flames that it was fanning, and the heat generated by the wind was enough to set fire to buildings before the fire ever reached them. Naturally, more and more people began to panic and evacuate their homes, as Ada Rumsey later recalled: "We hoped the river would prove a barrier to the flames, but this was not to be. Huge burning brands were carried by the wind, starting new fires in places…Christian [a servant to the family] had harnessed our two little black ponies to a phaeton belonging to my older sisters, and into this was put a clothes basket filled with silver and linen with some other things gathered up by Mother and Sister Meme. Also in the carriage were put the portraits of Father, Mother, and Grandfather Turner, and one or two other paintings…By this time houses were burning about us and our own house was on fire. The streets were filled with vehicles loaded with household goods, and with people staggering under big loads. Mother had waited for Father but was feeling that it would not be safe for us to stay much longer, when he appeared begrimed and tired. In his hand he carried a tin box of papers which he gave to Christian, who was just about to drive from the house with his load. Father said he did not know what was in the box, but it represented all the wealth he then possessed. So Christian drove off into the night with all that was left to us."

Sometime between midnight and 2:00 a.m., the mayor of the city, Roswell B. Mason, decided it was time to send to other communities for help, a fact underscored by the fact that the courthouse in which he had been working had been evacuated and caught fire. When the cupola containing the town's great bell collapsed at 2:20, the sound was so loud that it was heard a mile away, but by then, people across the city had to worry about the fact that much of the city was being consumed. William Gallagher noted, "At half-past two I was awakened by a tremendous knocking at my door, and on opening it I found one of my companions of the night before, who told me that Chicago was all on fire, that the Court House was gone, that all the business part of the city was in flames, and that he and his 'chum' were going down town. I dressed hastily, climbed to the roof, and saw a sight such as I never expect to see again, and which few men have had the privilege of witnessing…There was a strip of fire between two and three miles long, and a mile wide, hurried along by a wind that I have never seen excelled except by our September gale, sweeping through the business part of this city. We were situated where we could take in the whole at a sight, and such a view such a magnificent sight!"

Mayor Mason

Part of what drove the fire on through the night was "fire whirl," a meteorological situation that often occurs when large fires sweep across congested areas. As the overheated air rose into the sky, it came in contact with cooler air, which in turn caused it to cool suddenly and fall to earth. This created a sort of burning tornado that not only lit things on fire but also threw burning debris toward other areas, thereby starting new fires. When some of the debris kicked up by the fire whirl landed in a railroad car full of kerosene, it spread the blaze further and helped the fire jump the river again so that it began burning the north side of the city. According to Julia Lemos, "[A]bout five o'clock in the morning was woke up by a rumbling noise, so as I was awake I got up and threw open the shutters, I thought I was dreaming, the whole street was crowded with people, with hats and shawls on, a neighbor who stood in front of our house called to me, and said Mrs. Lemos, are you just getting up? I said yes, what is the matter? The sky was reflecting fire, she said the city has been burning all night, and the fire is coming to the north side, Well, that startled me, and I ran to the back room and called my father and mother up, I said the city is burning…by that time the fire was advancing on us, I wanted to leave the house, but father said, O, the wind will change. People were running in crowds past our house, I stood with my baby in my arms and the other children beside me, when a woman running past with three children, said to me, Madam, ain't you going to save those children, that started me, I went to Father and said I was going to leave at once…"

Chapter 5: The Water Runs Out

A picture of the ruins that appeared in *The New York Times*

A picture of the ruins on LaSalle St.

The Palmer House after the fire

"As thousands fled to the North Division, the fire pursued them. By 3:30 a.m., the roof collapsed on the Pumping Station at Chicago Avenue, effectively rendering any firefighting efforts hopeless. By noon on Monday the North Division fires had reached North Avenue and then continued the better part of a mile to Fullerton Avenue. Back in the South Division, the luxurious new Palmer House gave way, along with the offices of the Chicago Tribune, whose editors had exhorted the Common Council to raise the level of fire protection or face disaster. Tuesday morning a rain began to fall, and the flames finally died out, leaving Chicago a smoking, steaming ruin." - Bessie Bradwell Helmer

Although the situation was becoming increasingly hopeless, the firefighters continued to fight in an effort to save what they could. One of their main concerns was trying to keep the city's water supply flowing, not only to fight the fires but to ensure people still had water to drink. Unfortunately, the efforts were futile once a burning piece of wood from one building fell onto the roof of the facility and set it on fire. As the roof burned and fell through, pieces of it fell into the machinery and broke it, bringing the pumps to a halt. For the next few weeks, the citizens of the city were wholly dependent on the few older wells still in use around town for water.

Even worse, there was no more water with which to fight the fires. William Carter was among the first to see the damage: "Between one and two in the morning I went home, took Kate and the children to a place of safety, ordered the bedding and other things to be packed--went for teams--a difficult thing to find at that time of the night and then drove with all speed to the water works. My anxiety for the water works was due not more to save the buildings than to save a supply to the people to drink. It was too late, after going around in order to reach a spot of safety nearly five miles, I had to abandon the attempt and turned back almost in despair. The flames were rushing most frantically, leaping from block to block--whole squares vanishing as though they were gossamer."

Without water, the fire department quickly began trying to think of another way to stop the fire, and they decided to try to create some sort of fire break between where the fire was burning at the time and the rest of the city. In order to do this, they would have to take a very large chance by blowing up several buildings that were still standing. According the official report filed after the fire, "The engines had all been working on the West Side; and they could not reel-up six hundred feet of hose each, and cross the river, and get to work soon enough to prevent it spreading, literally, on the wings of the wind. Blowing up buildings in the face of the wind was tried, but without any benefit. The Court House and the Water Works, though a mile apart, were burning at the same time. Gunpowder was used in blowing up buildings, with good effect, the next day, in cutting off the fire at the extreme south end of it, and preventing it backing any further. After the Water Works burned, the firemen could do little good with their engines, except on the banks of the river."

From that point forward, the fire burned with no resistance, constantly perpetuating itself through the spread of ash and sparks. It spread across the city to areas that had not yet been burned, brought by the winds that continued to blow unabated through the night. Cassius Wicker later remembered, "Tops of all the buildings as well as the street were all a blaze. Chamber of Commerce and cupola of the C & N were a blaze, and flying embers and sheets of flame were born against the Skinner house, and falling would break into a thousand pieces, only to be born again into some basement, or further down the street by the perfect hurricane of a wind."

Though they had no water, the firefighters continued to fight on through the night by taking the hoses and pumps to the river and getting as much water from there as they could in order to keep up their battle against the spreading flames. These efforts were complicated by the fact that they had already lost a bunch of their equipment, and there was only so much they could do under those circumstances: "After the Water Works burned, the firemen could do little good with their engines, except on the banks of the river. They had lost seven thousand five hundred feet of hose and one steam fire engine. Two more engines had been in the repair shops…and, after daybreak, only one-half of our hose remained. This would not [allow] an engine conveying water very far from the river. The firemen and their officers were sober, and did all that men could do. They worked heroically to save the property of others, when their own houses were burning and their families fleeing from the flames. A large part of the Department had worked on Saturday night, and Sunday until 3 p.m.--eighteen hours' steady work,--and they were nearly exhausted when this fire commenced; but they responded to the call with alacrity and worked with all their remaining energy."

Chapter 6: Evacuation

Ruins from the interior of St. Paul's Church

The remains of the Lake-Side Publishing Company

"Chicago had a weakness for 'big things,' and liked to think that it was outbuilding New York. It did a great deal of commercial advertising in its house-tops. The faults of construction as well as of art in its great showy buildings must have been numerous. Their walls were thin, and were overweighted with gross and coarse misornamentation." – Frederick Olmsted

People were already terrified before word began to spread that the fire was out of control. However, while there was still water, there was hope that their brave firemen could get the fire under control, and that even if others' houses were burning, their own homes might be spared. Likewise, the Hebard's and the other visitors staying in the Palmer Hotel continued to hope for the best. After all, many had heard that its developer, Potter Palmer, called the hotel "The World's First Fireproof Building," but he was about to being proven terribly wrong. Mrs. Hebard later wrote, "About 11 P.M. I retired, but could not sleep, and it seemed not more than half an hour before there was a rapping at every door, and finally at ours, to which my husband responded very coolly, 'What's wanted?' 'Fire, sir!' was the answer, and the same moment we were on our feet. Our daughter was awakened, toilets soon made, and no time wasted in gathering together bags and shawls ready for departure. By this time my husband, who had stepped out to reconnoiter, returned, saying that everyone was stirring, and that he saw gentlemen dragging their own trunks down the stairs. The clerks at the office assured him there was no immediate danger, but they thought it well enough to be prepared. Then we all went once more to the seventh story, looked in vain for any evidence that the fire was decreasing, returned to our room, picked up our parcels, including the trunk (for no porters were to be found), descended to the office, paid our bill, and sat down to watch and wait. Finally, leaving our daughter in charge of the baggage, I went with my husband into the street, and around to the rear of the building where the fire was distinctly visible and apparently only two blocks from us."

At that point, the family soon reached the decision to join the many others thronging the streets and running away from the fire. While some either owned a carriage or cart, others tried in vain to hire one, but as the flames rose, so did the prices, so many were forced to make their way with their trunks and other belongings on their backs. Cassius Wicker was a bachelor and only responsible for his own safety, so he found his escape to be easier than that of many others: "My trunk was soon filled with the most valuable portion of my clothing, etc. and my hand bag packed for a camping out expedition, but all was done quickly and I assure you that I disposed of many an old garment, book and trinket that under other circumstances should not have [been] deserted in their old age. The bottle of brandy…was found while emptying my trunk of worthless trash and safely placed in the bag and it did good service the balance of that night and forenoon at Dick's, and many a stranger took courage from it. After helping my halls chamber girl down, and many another trunk before I could get my own down, I reached the street and started east as the heaviest portion of the fire was not yet there…everybody knew the town was doomed to destruction.

Not surprisingly, Wicker soon realized that the few worldly goods he was able to save were getting heavier by the minute. He explained, "Down to State Street, hailing every man or team for assistance, but all had…theirs to save. Dragging the trunks a block I would set down on it, only to be run over by others equally as anxious as I to get away from the devouring element. Would have given $10 for a rope five feet long--I never knew the value of such a rope until my back was nearly broken and hands so tired I could no longer stir the trunk." Fortunately, help soon arose from an unexpected corner, as he later related: "At last I came to a light wagon with a horse and obtained the assistance of a one-handed man to put the trunk into it, but the owner, or a man stronger than I claimed it. But my one-handed man would work for money and away we went, quite bravely until I could no longer lift my end. We rested more than we walked. Soon I could not stir my end and had a handkerchief through the handle and around my arm. This worked well until…both gave out entirely. Soon an Englishman, fleeing from the wrath,…in a large U.S. Express wagon, himself as motive power, with a few household goods and a sick wife came slowly along. I saw he was about exhausted and could not hold out much longer, so speedily compromised with him--adding our two loads together as well as our united strength, and the way we did the jackass business…"

Of course, only a small number of any person's belongings could be saved, so people made choices, leaving behind expensive oil paintings in favor of old daguerreotypes of dead relatives and wearing heavy wool coats instead of soft silk shawls. Likewise, beautiful churches were blown up in the hope of saving simple homes and offices. There would never be any way of knowing the full value of all the property lost, but there are a few records of some of the most mourned artwork and architecture. Wicker spoke of the losses, as well as the brave work of some who risked everything to save what they could: "The magnificent painting 16 by 32 feet of the Baron of Gillingsbury just behind the hotel was burned about this time. Hurrying to Dick's after seeing church after church, stone block after block blown up in vain endeavor to save what remained and after seeing the flames come from Dick's store, Pullman Palace Car Co. Building, and the Union Depot, we had just time to kick the fine pictures from their frames, load two wagons and be off up the avenue amid fire engines, everybody's last team and crowds of departing homeless people. Not until the flames came into the dining room and leaped over the roof did we leave the house. Never did I work as hard as for the last team--never did I see the avenue so full, to say nothing of crazy people. Never did I see such a wind carrying flames across the broad avenue."

Of course, even the best efforts of people to protect their valuables often failed. Many larger businesses during that era stored their receipts and record books in safes, many of which were supposed to be fireproof, so rather than carry large sums of money and bonds on them, many of the wealthier citizens of the town chose instead to lock these items, along with fine jewelry and other small but valuable possessions, in these safes and leave them behind. This strategy often proved to be a mistake, as Francis Test later explained: "The iron safes stood the heat well, but many were burned to a white heat; their contents were destroyed. I can safely say over two thirds of them were found to contain nothing but charred masses of what once were thousands in bonds and notes...Large safes may be seen walled in at a height of three and four stories. Some of the walls tell the place where a safe once was. The intense heat had made loose the bricks around them and they fell bursting or jammed in such a way that the fire searched out their contents. Many a man has awaited, buoyant with hope, the cooling and opening of his safe, and very many have been disappointed--thousands and thousands of dollars have been taken out charred and burned. I have seen safes completely melted and by one tap of the hammer would crumble like mortar. This fire has taught many lessons, especially in regard to iron safes and fire proof buildings."

The ruins of Wood's Museum

Picture of a poster from October 10 asking for food

"With the close of the fire, or rather conflagration, our troubles have not closed. Roughs and thieves from all parts of the country flocked here for plunder. Many fires have been started, but in most cases the party caught in the act has been shot on the spot. Their hopes were to burst open the safes, of which there are thousands through the burned district, but Gen. Sheridan promulgated a Death Proclamation to everybody found on the burnt district after dark. Thinking Milwaukee would be off their guard, many started for that city and we put them off the train when, for the sake of plunder, they attempted to throw a train off the track, but so far without success. Every block in the city is guarded strongly by the citizens. As an instance of our quiet times, Wednesday night while on watch between 8 & 2, I heard but 19 shots fired. Many, I hope, were false alarms, but it shows what little mercy is shown." - Cassius Wicker

As important as it was that the fire be put out, the city leaders also understood it was imperative for everyone's health and safety that order be restored. To that end, they made the following proclamation on Monday afternoon as the fire finally began to burn itself out:

❖ WHEREAS, In the Providence of God, to whose will we humbly submit, a terrible calamity has befallen our city, which demands of us our best efforts for the preservation of order and relief of suffering, be it known that the faith and credit of the City of Chicago is hereby pledged for the necessary expenses for the relief of the suffering.

❖ Public order will be preserved. The police and special police now being appointed will be responsible for the maintenance of the peace and protection of property.

❖ All officers and men of the Fire Department and Health Department will act as special policemen without further notice.

❖ The Mayor and Comptroller will give vouchers for all supplies furnished by the different relief committees.

❖ The headquarters of the City Government will be at the Congregational Church, corner of West Washington and Ann Streets.

❖ All persons are warned against any act tending to endanger property. Persons caught in any depredation will be immediately arrested.

❖ With the help of God, order and peace and private property will be preserved.

❖ The City Government and the committee of citizens pledge themselves to the community to protect them, and prepare the way for a restoration of public and private welfare.

❖ It is believed the fire has spent its force, and all will soon be well.

Damage on Washington St.

Though the fire finally burned itself out, aided by a light rain on Monday night, the city was still in great danger. The rain was not enough to thoroughly wet the buildings, and there was still no more water to be had. As Francis Test wrote, "We have the fire departments from all the larger cities in the West but the water has not been introduced into the pipes sufficient to put out the smallest fire. Water is being forced into the mains from the river by the fire engines. They have laid four inch mains above ground to a great distance on the South Side and the water is forced into them by the same means."

As a result, harsh laws against kindling any fire were put into effect. Not only were they enforced by the police officers and other government officials, they were also enforced by the citizens themselves, often with tragic results. As Test wrote, "The city is not strictly under martial law but it reminds me of the first days of the rebellion. Soldiers march our streets; the citizens are patrolling the squares; every alley is guarded and woe be to him that lights a match or smokes a cigar on the street after nightfall. Those who have this matter in charge will not permit any such thing. Fires in the house were prohibited for a long time but the rule is not so strictly observed now as it was. There have been a few men killed and I only wonder that the number is not greater, so intensely excited are the people. Some who have been shot deserved their fate, others were not guilty but indiscreet."

Fortunately, rain came again on Wednesday evening, giving people hope and much needed relief. Test continued, "It commenced raining last night and it is a Godsend. We have caught a supply of water, enough to do washing...The people of the West Side get water from Union Park. There is a small ornamental lake there, but this is fed by the water mains and was almost dipped out till the fire engines began forcing the water from the river into it. On the South Side they have the Lake and as I have said they are conveying water by means of a four inch main around the destroyed property and for a distance beyond."

Nonetheless, the water was only a drop in the bucket toward meeting the needs of the citizens, many of whom were in frightful condition and also needed food and shelter. As always during a disaster, there were those who wanted to take advantage of the situation with price gauging, but they were quickly and harshly dealt with. Test recalled, "I saw a farmer's wagon standing near a market store. It was loaded with bagged beans and a calf. He offered the beans at an exorbitant price and the calf he wanted $50.00 for. A crowd gathered around him and drove him from the city. It was with difficulty he got away unharmed."

Another need that had to be met was for care for the sick and injured. O.W. Clapp was charged with trying to organize locations suitable for medical care and later wrote, "It was there, and then I learned the usefulness of church basements for hospital uses, whereupon I ordered signs to be put on all churches south of the burnt district pointing to the next church basement south for food, beds and clothing. Within a few days all church basements on the south side acted as hospitals, as well as the hospitals and many schoolhouses and private homes." Fortunately, there were many others who just wanted to help, and Test praised these generous souls when he wrote, "Our sister cities are sending us food and everything we want. If it were not for this aid God knows what we should do. Provisions are plentiful and they are being properly disbursed."

In fact, a committee was soon organized to manage the donations being received. A poster informed the public, "J.W. Preston, Esq., President of the Board of Trade, is hereby authorized to receive on account of this Committee, all supplies for the relief of the destitute, and distribute the same to depots of supplies established in the city, under the control and upon the order of this Committee. He is also authorized to hire or press into service, if necessary, a sufficient number of teams to handle such supplies."

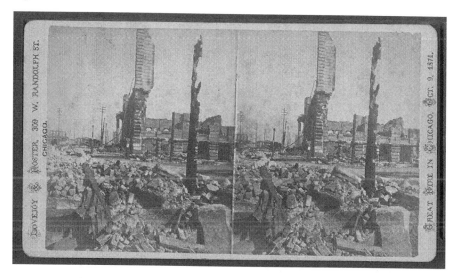

The remains of Chicago's Chamber of Commerce

Damage on Michigan Ave. in the northwestern section

"Having nothing of our own at stake, we could perhaps look on more coolly than some others. I remember being impressed at the time with the different phases of character so suddenly unveiled. The dear friends who so kindly sheltered us in our extremity, and who, for the last time, threw open those hospitable doors, not to friends merely, but to strangers as well--feeding the hungry, helping and sympathizing with those whose trials seemed greater than they could bear; those friends who looked on calmly as the devouring flames approached their beautiful dwelling, showing plainly that their treasure was laid up in a better country, where they looked for "a house not made with hands." Some came there, trembling and fearful, wholly broken-down, as it were, with their own grief; some came professedly to help--really to pilfer; but the majority were calm, earnest, resolute helpers…" - Mrs. Alfred Hebard

With food and water in place, the third concern for the surviving refugees was shelter, which was a dire situation since cities could not simply provide people places to live as they did with food. Furthermore, it was October, so the days and nights in Chicago were quite cold. Wicker described the first terrible night after the fire: "It's fearful. All down through Lake Park people were strung out on their few things saved, many of them fast asleep with the sand blowing over them…All day long, part of the night before and in many cases, Monday night, hundreds and thousands of people lay out on the sand in the wind strong enough to blow a chair left alone clear across the park. The air was so full of dust and sand that it was impossible to see the fire, and there, utterly exhausted, lay the lowly and the proud."

Unfortunately, at least one businessman thought he could make a profit off of people's misfortune, but according to Test, he quickly learned otherwise: "General Sheridan has control here now and this has done much to stay the confidence of the people. He is a little God here. Hotel and boarding housekeepers were trying to make money out of the misfortunes of the people. Sheridan went to one of our hotels, asked the proprietor what he asked for room and board per day. 'I am charging $10.00, sir. Will you register your name?' 'No sir, but I will inform you that if you cannot give room and board at $3.00 per day I can find someone that can. I suppose you understand that.'"

Fortunately, by Tuesday morning, help had been put in place for those left destitute by the fire. A public notice informed them, "The headquarters of the General Relief Committee are at the Congregational Church, corner of Washington and Ann streets. All of the public school buildings, as well as churches, are open for the shelter of persons who do not find other accommodations. When food is not found at such buildings, it will be provided by the committee on application headquarters." Moreover, the city did not have to provide shelter for everyone because some were able to find housing elsewhere in the area. Julia Lemos explained, "[F]ather told me that the government was giving free passes on the railroads, so people could go to their friends and that he could take us to New York to my aunt there. As all the firms I worked for were burned I knew it would be very long before I would have work to support the family, but might get work in New York, so I told father to get the pass and we would go. The next morning he went after the pass…Well how were we to get to the train for New York? There was no way--so the janitor of the church had a wagon and horse, and offered, if father would let him have the dog … he would take us to the train, in his wagon, so father arranged it, and he put our two trunks in the wagon then we got in…"

The railroads did indeed offer free passes to people, but they soon had to limit the policy to only women and children since the men were needed to help with repairing the city. The fire had destroyed more than 120 miles of sidewalk and 70 miles of road, and 2,000 lampposts were gone, leaving the city in eerie darkness each evening. A third of the city's buildings were gone, and more than 100,000 people left homeless.

Considering all the damage, the estimated death toll of close to 300 was surprisingly low, and Frederick Olmsted found the number so low that he mentioned it in his writings: "That the number should be small can only be accounted for by the fact that there was an active volunteer rear-guard of cool-headed Christians, who often entered and searched houses to which they were strangers, dragging out their inmates sometimes by main force, and often when some, caught unawares, were bewildered, fainting, or suffocating." He continued praising those left in Chicago, writing, "For a time men were unreasonably cheerful and hopeful; now, this stage appears to have passed. In its place there is sternness; but so narrow is the division between this and another mood, that in the midst of a sentence a change of quality in the voice occurs, and you see that eyes have moistened. I had partly expected to find a feverish, reckless spirit, and among the less disciplined classes an unusual current setting towards turbulence, lawlessness, and artificial jollity, such as held in San Francisco for a long time after the great fire there--such as often seizes seamen after a wreck. On the contrary, Chicago is the soberest and the most clear headed city I ever saw. I have observed but two men the worse for liquor; I have not once been asked for an alms, nor have I heard a hand-organ. The clearing of the wreck goes ahead in a driving but steady, well-ordered way. I have seen two hundred brick walls rising, ten thousand temporary houses of boards, and fifty thousand piles of materials lifting from the ruins…"

There was a good reason why Olmsted observed so little drunkenness; during the days following the fire, the city's first order was "that no liquor be sold in any Saloon," and the city later decreed, "All saloons are ordered to be closed at 9 P.M. every day for one week, under a penalty of forfeiture of license."

Chapter 9: Protection

"There was a crowd in the middle of the street dragging a man along with a rope around his neck, they were going to hang him, he had been caught setting fire for robbery, that frightened me, and I said we will leave Chicago at once, I would be afraid to have my children on the street. The second night at the church every one was asleep at midnight, but on account of my baby being restless, I woke up, and saw a rough looking man coming in the church door, I pretended to be asleep but watched him, he laid down in a pew for a while, then he rose up and looked about to see if he was observed, a man laid asleep in the next pew, and he reached over and was just taking his watch, when I set up and the thief started and laid down again, I pretended to wait on baby, but whispered to mother to tell father, which she did, and as father was an old soldier and had a gun, he with several others were appointed a guard in the church, he went to the others and called them, and they closed about the man and took him to a guardhouse they had about there." - Julia Lemos

Determined to protect the citizens in his community, Mayor Mason issued a notice as the fire was dying down that the city would be divided into districts and that each district would recruit 500 citizens to act as Special Policemen. Furthermore, he announced, "The Military are invested with full Police power, and will be respected and obeyed in their efforts to preserve order." In effect, he declared martial law and put General Philip Sheridan, a Union hero during the Civil War, in charge of keeping order in the city. Charles Holden later wrote, "For two weeks Sheridan oversaw a de facto martial law of dubious legitimacy implemented by a mix of regular troops, militia units, police, and a specially organized 'First Regiment of Chicago Volunteers.' They patrolled the streets, guarded the relief warehouses, and enforced curfews and other regulations. John DeKoven, cashier of the Merchants' National Bank of Chicago, wrote to his wife of his experience as a sentry, 'I have not had my clothes off for a week, the city is patrolled every night, you should have seen me last night patrolling our alley with a loaded revolver in my hand looking for incendiaries for there are many about.' Illinois Governor Richard Oglesby, among others, strongly questioned whether such measures were justified and legal, but the calming effect of Mason's actions in the days right after the fire was evident, especially among the well-to-do. Former Lieutenant-Governor William Bross, part owner of the Tribune, later recollected his response to the arrival of Sheridan's soldiers: 'Never did deeper emotions of joy overcome me. Thank God, those most dear to me and the city as well are safe.'"

Illustration depicting the ruins of the National Bank of Chicago

Sheridan

Unfortunately, the citizen police officers were not thoroughly trained in handling difficult situations like the police often encountered. In fact, they were not really trained at all. Many were former Union soldiers who had fought in the Civil War and as such had developed a certain willingness to shoot at a fellow American that many past and future generations would find hard to understand. Others had fought in the Indian Wars and had not fired a gun in decades. Still others had never been in any kind of organized conflict and had no clue how to give and take orders. The only thing that the mayor could hope for was that most were armed with some sort of common sense.

O.W. Clapp was one of those deputized, and he made the following observation about his service, which centered primarily on the first wave of food distribution: "Mayor Mason then clothed me with a lead pencil order on the back of an old envelope and a Policeman's star and a verbal order to act on my own responsibility and not bother him. I proceeded to ask the views of those I thought my peers in this emergency and visited certain sections of the south side driving through parts of the burnt district...Next morning ... I went to the Plymouth Congregational Church, corner Wabash Ave. and Eldridge Court and found Rev. Wm. Alvin Bartlett at breakfast and applied to him for men in the basement of his church to go with me to the Warehouse and help unload cars and load wagons... The Doctor at once went to the basement of his church, mounting a chair called for recruits to aid the distribution. About 20 men volunteered... Coming out we saw one of Farwells, and one of Fields big truck wagons. I ordered the driver to take these men on their trucks to the 18th St. warehouse, near the river. They rebelled, but soon repented being persuaded by the minister and men and my showing of a police star."

As the weeks wore on, there was more and more to protect and distribute. Towns from around the state and cities from around the country began to send donations to Chicagoans. New York City send food, clothing and $450,000 in cash, while Milwaukee, St. Louis, Cleveland, Buffalo and Cincinnati provided hundreds of thousands of dollars worth of money and goods. Even London, on the other side of the world, sent more than £7,000 to Chicago. To his credit, Mason was sensitive to the need to manage these donations well and formed yet another committee. As Holden pointed out, "The Relief and Aid Society's fire activities were considerably more long-lived, extending into 1874. Dividing the city into districts, the Society opened offices and supply depots connected by telegraph. It separated its work into different areas--contributions, shelter, employment, transportation, distribution, and health--each overseen by a designated committee. The Society not only distributed food and clothing, but also made available the materials for several thousand simple 'shelter houses,' erected four barracks in different places throughout the city for the homeless poor, helped secure necessary tools and appliances to skilled workers, and vaccinated tens of thousands of Chicagoans against smallpox. Its work was a model of a new kind of 'scientific' charity, conducted by paid professionals carrying out the policies of an executive board."

CHEER UP.

In the midst of a calamity without parallel in the world's history, looking upon the ashes of thirty years' accumulations, the people of this once beautiful city have resolved that CHICAGO SHALL RISE AGAIN

Part of an article in *The Chicago Tribune* after the fire

"You ask whether it is in the power of man adequately to guard against such calamities-- whether other great cities are as much exposed as was Chicago. All the circumstances are not established with sufficient accuracy for a final answer, and one cannot, in the present condition of affairs, make full enquiries of men who must be best informed; but to such preliminary discussion as is in order, I can only offer a certain contribution. (…) No one can be sure that with reasonably solid brick walls, reasonably good construction, and honest architecture, this fire could, once under strong headway, with the wind that was blowing, have been stopped at any point in its career, even by good generalship, directing a thoroughly well-drifted and disciplined soldierly force of fireman and police. But that the heat thrown forward would have been less intense, the advance of the fire less rapid, the destruction of buildings less complete, the salvage of their contents greater, and the loss of life smaller, may be assumed with confidence." - Frederick Olmsted

Fanny Boggs Lester was 11 when Chicago burned, and she recorded her memories in a letter written about 75 years later: "Opposite us on the S.E. corner of Michigan Ave. and Twenty-third was a vacant lot. When we looked out in the morning it was filled with refugees from the hotels with their belongings in bags, sheets and pillow cases. In front of our house was a hearse filled with baggage and on the driver's seat a man with his marble mantle clock. I remember my mother saying, 'I certainly would not have chosen that heavy thing to carry,' so as one of the letters said 'there were amusing things too.' I remember my mother with others feeding these sufferers, in the Michigan Ave. Baptist Church which was two doors from us, and for many following weeks, because a distributing center to give out clothing and food that came so generously from many places. The danger from incendiary fires made my father and the other residents of our blocks watch night after night. One was discovered near us. I to help, got my new shoes and put all the silver and napkins in these and was ready to go. For weeks we had to use candles which mother put in bottles with water in them and card-board to catch the wax. When my father let me ride down with him to see the wreck the cedar blocks of the pavement were still smoking in many places which our horse did not like..."

As is always the case with a tragedy, the story is not complete until someone has been blamed. While this seems cruel and mean-spirited, there is also a practical reason for establishing blame, because if people can determine what went wrong in the situation, there is hope that corrections can be made in the future and that such a hardship will not have to be experienced again. One of the first reports issued about what could have prevented the fire, or at least minimized its damage, came from those at the forefront of fighting it. The official report of the board of the Chicago Fire Department observed, "We believe that had the buildings on the West Side, where the fire commenced, been built of brick or stone, with safe roofings (the buildings need not have been fire-proof) the fire could have been stopped without great danger, and certainly would not have crossed the river. After it did cross, the wooden cornices, wooden signs of large size, the cupolas, and the tar and felt roofs, which were on most of the best buildings, caused their speedy destruction, and aided greatly in spreading the conflagration." The board then went on to add, "The single set of pumping works, upon which the salvation of the city depended, were roofed with wood, had no appliance by which water could be raised to the roof in case of fire, and was one of the earliest buildings to burn in the North Division."

In order to bolster its case, the board went on to point out, "The Board of Police have, year by year, in annual reports to the Mayor and Common Council, endeavored to point out the great defects of the manner in which our city was being built up. We advised and entreated before such an immense amount of combustibles was piled around the heart of the city. We reported mansard and tar roofs to be unsafe; that the water supply was insufficient; that our fire hydrants were twice too far apart; that we ought to have Fire Department cisterns at the intersections of the streets, so that we should always have water at fires; that we ought to have floating fire engines, with powerful pumps, in the river, to enable the firemen to wet down fifteen hundred feet on either side of the river or its branches; that wooden cornices were an abomination; that the Holly system of pumping the water and sending it through the pipes, with a pressure of forty pounds on ordinary occasions, with power to increase it to one hundred pounds in case of fire, would give us four sets of pumping works in different parts of the city, and not leave us to the mercy of chance, or, accident, with a single set."

Of course, the changes suggested in the report would have been expensive, and then as now, small local governments were reluctant to spend the money to make the upgrades. Also, the Civil War had ended a mere six years earlier, and the entire country was in the midst of a post-war economic crisis that even affected growing cities like Chicago. That said, the report was quick to point out the flaw in the "costs too much" excuse: "We showed that the four sets of Holly works could be built for less than one year's interest on the cost of the present Water Works, and, when built, would admit of the dispensing with every engine in the Fire Department where the water was in the street, allowing us to get rid of most of the horses and all the engines of the Department, and to reduce the number of men one-half--saving two-thirds of the expense of the Fire Department, and making it as efficient as it would be with one hundred steam fire engines."

Having gotten the readers' attention, the authors of the report then went in for the kill, writing: "None of these things was noticed by the mayor, the Common Council, or the newspapers. No heed being paid to our suggestions, so far as any improvement of our plan of extinguishing fires was concerned, the only thing we could do was to ask for an increase of the engine companies, in order that we might be prepared as well as possible to contend with the great fires to which we were and are still liable." They closed with a summary of their concerns: "Our engines have always been too few in number and too far apart. The Fire Department should be very much enlarged, or the system of putting out fires by steam engines be abandoned. If the citizens do not believe this now, they will after the next great fire sweeps out of existence the greater portion of the wooden city which now remains."

This time, the city leaders listened. Within weeks of the fire, committees began to draft new laws concerning where and how new buildings could be built. They also consulted fire prevention expert Arthur C. Ducat and others on how to reform the fire department. Before long, the Chicago Fire Department earned a reputation for being one of the best fire departments in the United States.

Meanwhile, Gordon Hubbard, who had sheltered the Hebard's and many others until his own home burned, threw his money and efforts into rebuilding the city. In fact, he ordered lumber delivered to town before the last fire had even gone out. Francis Test also tried to assure those he was writing to: "The heart of our city is gone, but our business men are not discouraged. Soon we will begin again. Even now over the smoldering ruins they are placing new buildings. Our houses may be burned but our energies are just the same, they cannot be destroyed. It looks like rain tonight. The clouds are very dark and on these the light from the burning coal heaps reflect a living red that is surely visible for miles. We have the fire departments from all the larger cities in the West but the water has not been introduced into the pipes sufficient to put out the smallest fire. Water is being forced into the mains from the river by the fire engines. They have laid four inch mains above ground to a great distance on the South Side and the water is forced into them by the same means."

Mayor Mason, who saw the city through its darkest days, stayed on to help with the rebuilding, but not as mayor. He was soon replaced in office by his successor, Joseph Medill, and less than two weeks after the fire, he issued his last order related to the incident: "In view of the recent appalling public calamity, the undersigned, Mayor of Chicago, hereby earnestly recommends that all the inhabitants of this city do observe Sunday, October 29, as a special day of humiliation and prayer; of humiliation for those past offenses against Almighty God, to which these severe afflictions were doubtless intended to lead our minds; of prayer for the relief and comfort of the suffering thousands in our midst; for the restoration of our material prosperity, especially for our lasting improvements as a people in reverence and obedience to God. Nor should we even, amidst our losses and sorrows, forget to render thanks to Him for the arrest of the devouring fires in time to save so many homes, and for the unexampled sympathy and aid which has flowed in upon us from every quarter of our land, and even from beyond the seas."

Picture of a sculpture commemorating the site where the fire started

Bibliography

Bales, Richard F. (2002). *The Great Chicago Fire and the Myth of Mrs. O'Leary's Cow*. Jefferson, NC.: McFarland.

Chicago and the Great Conflagration – Elias Colbert and Everett Chamberlin, 1871, 528 pp.

"Who Caused the Great Chicago Fire? A Possible Deathbed Confession" – by Anthony DeBartolo, *Chicago Tribune*, October 8, 1997 and "Odds Improve That a Hot Game of Craps in Mrs. O'Leary's Barn Touched Off Chicago Fire" – by Anthony DeBartolo, *Chicago Tribune*,

March 3, 1998

"History of the Great Fires in Chicago and the West". – Rev. Edgar J. Goodspeed, D.D., 677 pp.

The Great Conflagration – James W. Sheahan and George P. Upton 1871, 458 pp.

Smith, Carl (1995). *Urban Disorder and the Shape of Belief: The Great Chicago Fire, the Haymarket Bomb, and the Model Town of Pullman.* Chicago, Ill.: University of Chicago Press.

"Mrs. O'Leary's Comet: Cosmic Causes of the Great Chicago Fire" by Mel Waskin (Jan 1985)

Made in the USA
Lexington, KY
07 June 2015